People Who Have Helped the World

Library

LOUIS BRAILLE

by Beverley Birch

Picture Credits

Bridgeman Art Library, pp. 8-9, 50-51 — Musée Picardy, Amiens, p. 9, — National Gallery of Capidomonte, Naples, p. 18, — Victoria and Albert Museum, pp. 4, 27; Chevojon Frères, p. 44; Exley Photographic Library, p. 21, — Nick Birch, cover, pp. 10, 12 (both), 16 (below), 29, 30, 35 (both), 37 (both), 42, 43 (both), 47, 55 (both), 57; Fine Art Photographic Library, pp. 16 (above), 22, 46; Giraudon, pp. 22, 52; Alan Hutchinson Library — Maurice Harvey, p. 58 (left), — Juliet Highet, p. 58 (right); Rex Features Ltd., pp. 38, 59 (above); Roger-Viollet, pp. 28, 56 (below); Ann Ronan Picture Library, pp. 14, 15, 24, 25, 48, 56 (above); Royal National Institute for the Blind, pp. 6, 7, 33, 36, 41; Science Photo Library: Eunice Harris, p. 59 (below).

The publishers owe special thanks to Patricia Beattie and Alberta Lonergan of the American Foundation for the Blind, New York, and Bonnie Peterson of the National Federation of the Blind, Milwaukee.

North American edition first published in 1989 by
Gareth Stevens, Inc.
7317 West Green Tree Road
Milwaukee, WI 53223 USA

First published in the United Kingdom in 1989 with
an original text © 1989 by Exley Publications Ltd.
Additional end matter © 1989 by Gareth Stevens, Inc.

Library of Congress Cataloging-in-Publication Data

Birch, Beverley.
    Louis Braille / by Beverley Birch.
       p.   cm. -- (People who have helped the world)
    Includes index.
    ISBN 0-8368-0097-4
    1. Braille, Louis, 1809-1852--Juvenile literature. 2. Teachers,
Blind--France--Biography--Juvenile literature. 3. Blind--Printing
and writing systems--Juvenile literature. I. Title. II. Series.
HV1624.B65B57   1989
686.2'12'0924--dc19
[B]   89-4275

Series conceived and edited by Helen Exley
Picture research: Karen Gunnell
Editorial: Margaret Montgomery
Editor, U.S.: Valerie Weber
Editorial assistant, U.S.: Scott Enk

Printed in Hungary

1 2 3 4 5 6 7 8 9 94 93 92 91 90 89

LOUIS BRAILLE

The inventor of a way to read and write that has helped millions of blind people communicate with the world

by Beverley Birch

Gareth Stevens Children's Books
MILWAUKEE

Louis' quest

No sound could be heard in the darkness except the deep, regular breathing of sleeping boys, the creak of a rusty iron bed, the occasional rustle of blankets, and if you listened carefully, a faint, muffled knocking.

One boy was not asleep. He was sitting up, covers hunched around him against the damp chill of the night, intent on something balanced across his knees. It was a small board covered with paper, and he was pressing down on it — a short, punching movement of his hand, a pause, then another string of sharp, downward punches.

He was not bothered by working in the darkness. Nor should he have been, for darkness or light made no difference to him. He could not see it. Nor could he see the sleeping boys around him, nor the beds, nor the windows, nor the door. Nor, for that matter, could he see the board he held steadily on his knees, nor the quick movements of his hand.

He was blind. He had been blind for almost as long as he could remember. His companions in that dark room, all those quietly sleeping boys in their narrow beds on either side, were also blind. But while they slept, he was almost dropping with fatigue. It would be many hours before he allowed himself the luxury of sleep. His task was not done yet, and there weren't enough hours in the day for him to finish it. On he went, steadily punching the pointed instrument that he held down against the board and paper. He listened to the muffled knocking sound that his movement made.

This was not the first time fourteen-year-old Louis Braille had spent the hours of the night hunched over his board and paper. If this time wasn't enough, he would get up early to do more work before the day began, before lessons ate into his free time.

Opposite: In a dank, crowded neighborhood in Paris, much like the one shown here, a thirteen-year-old boy began to develop a unique method of writing and reading for blind people. His system has since become the international alphabet for blind people and is named after him — braille.

A	B	C	D
•	• •	• •	• • •
E	**F**	**G**	**H**
• •	• • •	• • • •	• • •
I	**J**	**K**	**L**
• •	• • •	• •	• • •
M	**N**	**O**	**P**

• •
 	
•
	• •
	  •
	•
		•
		  •
		•
			• •
			•
			•

Q	**R**	**S**	**T**
• • • • •	• • • •	• • •	• • • •
U	**V**	**W**	**X**
• • •	• • • •	• • •	• • • •
Y	**Z**		

• •
  •
• •
	•
	  •
	• •		

and	for	of	the
• • • • • •	• • • • • •	• • • • •	• • • •

The genius of Braille's system was in its ease and simplicity. With the touch of a single fingertip, a blind person could recognize each letter of the alphabet.

He had been working at this task for months. He had even taken it to his home during his school vacation. He sat through the long summer on a sunny slope or the farmhouse steps, while his family smiled. Villagers passed by and nodded to one another, "Ah, there's young Louis at his pinpricks again!"

Pinpricks on a piece of paper were all they were to those around Louis. But to him, they were everything. Others watched his activity with amusement and affection. For when all was said and done, they said to themselves, what could a blind boy be doing so seriously that was important? And they shook their heads at his misfortune, wishing him and his game well.

Pinpricks they were, but pinpricks destined to become the international alphabet for blind people, the key to the door of reading, writing, learning, and culture for blind people everywhere. Once opened, that door could never again be slammed shut against them. Blind people would never again be locked into darkness, unable to learn.

Within sixty years, the world would see the pinpricks of fourteen-year-old Louis Braille as one of the greatest gifts one person could give to others.

A determined child

In that damp dormitory in Paris in 1823, Louis Braille could not foresee the extent of his achievement. He knew only that some way must be found for blind people to read and write as easily as sighted people do. He knew there must be a way for blind people to share in the world's knowledge and to take part in expanding that knowledge.

And he also knew that a way could be found. It was a belief born from his youth and from his own passion for learning. It was born, too, from his energy and hope that would not allow him to be easily discouraged. He knew the difficulties of blind people did not have to be made worse by their being unable to read and having to depend on others. He knew they did not have to be cut off from a normal life by a thousand barriers.

It was possible to find a way. Louis knew it. He would not rest until he found it.

"Access to communication in the widest sense is access to knowledge. . . . We do not need pity, nor do we need to be reminded that we are vulnerable. We must be treated as equals — and communication is the way we can bring this about."
Louis Braille, 1841

The saddler's son from Coupvray

Louis Braille had not always been blind. For the first three years of his life, he had his sight. He had filled the family house with the explorations and curiosity of any young child. His adventures amused his brother and sisters — seventeen-year-old Louis-Simon, nineteen-year-old Catherine-Joséphine, and fourteen-year-old Marie-Céline.

Louis brought a particular glow of warmth to his mother and father. He had come into their lives late, when his mother, Monique, was already forty-one and his father, Simon-René, forty-four. At Louis' birth, Simon-René had proudly declared that the boy would be the support and the companion of his old age.

A country childhood

Louis was born on January 4, 1809, in the village of Coupvray, about twenty-five miles (40 km) east of Paris, France. Coupvray was close to the great, wide, flat expanse of the wheat-growing lands of the La Brie district. Nestling on the slopes of the gentle, wooded hills above the valleys of the Marne River, Coupvray was a bustling, rural village. It boasted a tailor, a ropemaker, a weaver, a locksmith, a doctor, a pharmacist, and a midwife.

But its people were mainly farmers, winegrowers, and artisans whose skills were vital to a farming

community: a blacksmith, a wheelwright, and Louis' father, the village saddler and harnessmaker. His was a highly skilled trade much in demand in those days of horse-drawn wagons and carriages. Simon-René's father had also been a saddler, and Simon-René hoped both Louis and Louis-Simon would continue in the family trade.

It was a simple, ordinary, busy life. The family owned the farmhouse and Simon-René's workshop, as well as seven-and-a-half acres (3 ha) of land and vineyards in the village. It kept them fully occupied and provided a reasonable supply of food throughout

the year. They were not rich. But they did not lack the essentials of life nor good friends in their hard-working, tightly knit community. A weekly market day drew in people from other villages. There were also four fairs each year and the highlight of the year, the grape harvest and its celebrations.

The family house stood on a road named Chemin des Buttes. But in recognition of the inventor who spent his early childhood there, the road was later renamed Rue Louis Braille. The stone farmhouse squatted sturdily below its huge roof, with its dark, leaded windows, massive oak doors, and vast chimney. Here Louis would play or chatter to his mother as she went about her work. When Louis grew bored, he could visit his father in the workshop across the yard.

What a fascinating place this was! The shop was full of bridles, reins, and straps, rich with the smell of oiled leather. Heavy cone-shaped blocks of wood for the horses' collars stood in the corners. And in the middle of it all was the sturdy bench that his father leaned over to cut and shape leather for harnesses and saddles. There was an array of shining tools — knives for cutting the leather and awls for making holes, all polished and razor sharp.

The plunge into darkness

There are no written records from that time of the blinding of Louis Braille. Nor do we know exactly when it took place in that year of 1812. The story has been drawn together from different people's memories — the rest we have to imagine for ourselves. But it is not difficult to picture the curious three-year-old, intent on copying the exciting tasks he saw his father doing daily, climbing on to the high wood bench. Perhaps it happened when Simon-René was outside for a moment in the yard, talking to a farmer about repairs needed for some harness.

One can imagine Louis' seizing a piece of leather, reaching for an awl or knife, and eagerly imitating those precise, intricate movements of his father's skilled hands. But in the chubby hands of a three-year-old, the sharp instrument of craft and skill was merely a crude but efficient instrument of destruction.

Opposite: While we do not know whether Braille was blinded by an awl or a knife, this painting by A. Harfort shows Braille reaching for a saddler's knife. The painting now hangs in his father's workshop in Coupvray, where the Braille family home is preserved as a museum.

11

Above: The workshop and saddler's tools belonging to Braille's father, Simon-René Braille.

Right: The steps to the Braille cellar.

We know of a scream from the workshop, the sobbing boy found with blood pouring down his face. It seems that his hands had slipped and the tool had sliced into his eye.

His panic-stricken parents did all they could. They brought fresh water and white linen to bandage the bleeding eye. An old woman of the village who understood the healing properties of herbs brought lily water to wash it. They put a dressing on his eye and tried to soothe the frightened child.

Permanent blindness

Louis stopped crying, the blood stopped flowing, and the family consulted the local doctor at once. But in those days, doctors did not understand the causes and control of infection.

It was long before the work of the scientist Louis Pasteur taught them about germs and how infection develops and is carried — on hands and bandages and in the air. It was more than a hundred years before the British researcher Alexander Fleming discovered penicillin, the first antibiotic that could cure infections by killing dangerous germs without harming a patient.

Helplessly, doctors and family alike watched Louis' injured eye become red and puffy. The eyelid grew swollen and looked bruised. Louis rubbed his eye to clear his vision. But whatever infection that had taken hold now spread to the other eye. Objects around him seemed blurred, as though he were looking at them through a mist.

One can imagine his becoming more clumsy and more cautious. His family must have slowly adjusted to the sounds of the bumps and crashes when he dropped his plate as he stretched to put it on the table, when he collided with the furniture or missed his footing on the cellar stairs. These were the symptoms of the creeping darkness that descended permanently over Louis.

We are told of visits to an eye doctor in the nearby town of Meaux, but everything was useless. Day by day, his vision gradually faded. Nothing could be done to save the eyesight of Louis Braille. He would never see from either eye again.

Louis adapts

Gradually, Louis must have changed. Sighted children learn to imitate the actions of those around them, to observe how others move their eyes, mouth, hands, and head. But these memories would slowly recede from Louis' mind. His face grew quieter and more withdrawn, his head taking on the forward and sideways tilt he carried throughout his life.

His whole body focused now on replacing his sight with his other senses. He began to recognize the sounds of his footsteps on different surfaces, the varying echoes of his voice as it bounced off walls, doors, and furniture. He learned to recognize the noises of the street outside, the rumble of cart wheels, the jingle of his father carrying harnesses, the murmur of people's voices, and the barking of dogs. They filled his world with the sound and texture of things he could no longer see.

For centuries, most blind people rarely ventured from their homes and families or depended on others to give them charity because they could not earn a living. A few blind people might hope for a few coins playing music, like the musicians in this picture.

And we can imagine the busy household finding tasks for Louis to do. His family found that he had an amazing ability to tell what things were by just touching them, as if his fingers had already replaced his eyesight. He was able to sort shapes and widths of leather for his father and later to make fringes for the harness. He could sort vegetables and eggs for his mother and sisters as they rushed to prepare for the weekly market.

Gradually Louis forgot what it had ever been like to see. He became a little more adventurous in his world of darkness. He gained more skill at knowing exactly which dog had barked, whose cart had rolled up to the workshop, who had called to him cheerily. He no longer bumped and crashed around the house because now he knew it by sound as well as touch.

An occupied country

This unbroken pattern of life in Coupvray did not last long. In early 1814, bad news shook the citizens of Coupvray. The previous October, the combined forces of the Austrians, Russians, and Prussians had defeated France's army, led by Emperor Napoleon Bonaparte. The French army was now in full retreat. The troops were short of food and falling back in disorder to the French capital, Paris.

The official records of Coupvray tell us something of the progress of Napoleon's retreat and the enemy army's advance across France. On January 2, 1814, the army instructed Coupvray to provide 275 bushels of oats for the retreating Napoleonic troops. On January 23, they asked for 132 more bushels. On January 28, they ordered 1,200 bundles of hay and eight cows. On February 8, the baker had to make 706 loaves of bread for the army. On February 20, the army seized all the horses of the district and then a dozen cows.

By April, the people of Coupvray had their own evidence of the defeat of Napoleon. He was forced to abdicate, and King Louis XVIII replaced him as ruler of France. Later that month, soldiers of the Imperial Russian Army entered Coupvray, and a new series of demands began — food, horses, cows, hay, oats, and wagons for the occupation army.

There were few careers possible for blind people during Braille's lifetime. At best, they could learn some simple craft like the basketry being done by this blind boy.

Enemy Prussian soldiers billeted with the Braille household and with others in Coupvray. Now Louis' life echoed with the harsh voices of strangers and the new footsteps he had to learn to recognize. His father's workshop bustled with foreign cavalrymen bringing in harnesses for repair. And always, there was the hushed talk of events he could not fully understand. The adults around him were worried, their conversations punctuated by sudden silences when a Prussian soldier came near enough to hear.

Russians, Prussians, Bavarians, and more Russians. Over the two-year occupation, Louis' family had sixty-four different soldiers staying in their house. Louis was seven before they left in the summer of 1816. Now the villagers could take up the threads of normal life again. They could try to repair the fabric of their community and recover from the hardship of the years of army occupation.

A friend

The year Louis turned six, his third year of blindness, was the start of a new era for him. It was the year that a new parish priest came to Coupvray.

The first task of the Abbé Jacques Palluy was to visit the families of his parish. He soon got to know the Braille household and Louis. Within weeks, the priest and child had settled into a pattern of easy friendship and companionship.

Seated in good weather in the church garden or in colder weather in the priest's house, Palluy began a series of lessons with Louis. He told stories from the Bible and taught the blind child to recognize the different scents and textures of flowers and to identify the sounds of different birds and animals. He talked to him about the seasons of the year and the changing pattern of the day.

Fascinated and excited, Louis listened. He began to recognize the smells and bird songs of the dawn and to feel the creeping cool of the evening before it arrived. And as their friendship grew, Palluy also awakened in Louis a deep religious faith that was to remain with him for the rest of his life.

Louis starts school

Louis reached school age. At the nearby village school, there was by now another newcomer to Coupvray, a young, dedicated, and enthusiastic schoolmaster, Antoine Bécheret.

No sooner had Bécheret started teaching than Palluy went to see him about Louis. Never mind that most people would say there was no point in giving a blind boy lessons! Never mind that a blind boy could not read or write! Louis was alert, intelligent, and interested in everything around him. He would surely benefit from being able to listen to the lessons and from sharing the school life of the other children of the village!

Bécheret agreed. New to his profession, he was not totally convinced that teaching a blind child was useless. Nor was he afraid that the authorities in charge of the school would object to his educating a blind person, someone unlikely to use his education or to be taught a trade.

Opposite, above: Defeated at the Battle of Leipzig in October 1813, French Emperor Napoleon Bonaparte retreated toward Paris, seizing supplies from villages like Coupvray. In the early months of 1814, news of the battles to the east and south of Coupvray upset the villagers. Then came the news of Napoleon's abdication. This picture shows the French in retreat after their final defeat by the British and the Prussians at Waterloo in June 1815.

Opposite, below: The countryside surrounding Coupvray.

Because most blind people were uneducated, sighted people for centuries had seen their blindness as a form of stupidity, a punishment, or an occasion for mockery. This painting by Pieter Brueghel portrays the blind leading the blind and shows the kind of caricature made of the subject.

So Louis set off each day with one of his friends for the village school. Sitting on his bench in the front, close to the teacher where he could hear every word, Louis drank in the lessons as though he could not learn enough.

He seemed to understand and memorize what was said instantly. He seemed never to forget what he had heard. It was almost as though the events of history and the places and peoples of geography opened up a world of the imagination that took the place of the world of sight that he had lost.

From the beginning, he was at the head of his class. Even at this early stage, he was determined not to accept the idea that his blindness must be a prison without books. It would not mean a world without the chance to communicate with his friends, record his thoughts, or write his notes.

For example, a friend of the Brailles recalled that Louis' father hammered nails into wood in the shape of the letters of the alphabet. Louis taught himself to recognize these by touch. There are other stories that

say his father cut the shapes of letters out of leather. Another story tells that his sister Catherine-Joséphine made letters from straw for him.

What future for Louis?

But dreams in the head of young Louis were one thing. The real prospects for Louis as an adult were quite another. His parents worried about his future when they would no longer be able to care for him and provide for him.

There was little hope for blind people in those days. They could not study the same way sighted people could, so it was usually impossible to learn a trade or do work of any kind. How else could a person expect to earn a living?

Most blind people had to depend entirely on others for everything they needed. Their relatives would care for them if they were rich and could make provision for them.

But if their relatives were poor or cast them out, blind people often had nothing. Many had to beg on

A school like the one in Coupvray that Braille attended. It was unusual for blind children in France and other countries to go to school with sighted children.

"Homeless blind people of all ages roamed the streets of most large towns, and even well-educated men and women seemed to find it amusing to watch them groping their way and bumping into buildings. They would throw things at them or trip them up, and then burst into laughter."

Norman Wymer,
The Inventors

the streets for money and food. And because blind people were so often uneducated, sighted people commonly interpreted their blindness as stupidity. They treated them like outcasts, at best to be housed in an asylum out of harm's way.

So what was to become of Louis? As long as there were members of his family to care for him, he would lack neither love, food, clothing, nor shelter.

But there must be more to life for him than this! Palluy was determined that no effort should be spared to find some way of settling young Louis on a more fruitful path. He began questioning everyone he knew for information that would help Louis.

A special school in Paris

There are several different stories told about how Louis' family heard of the special school for blind children in Paris. It seems most likely that his teacher Bécheret remembered hearing about it. Spurred on by this discovery, Palluy set out to find out more.

We know that he decided to approach the lord of the manor up in his grand chateau. The Marquis d'Orvilliers was a nobleman who had several times helped needy people in the village. The priest hoped the marquis would hear him with sympathy.

He was not disappointed. The marquis had noticed Louis in church on Sundays. He listened with interest to Palluy's plea for help in the matter of Louis Braille's future.

The marquis himself also knew of the school for blind children in Paris. He remembered that he had once met the founder, a man named Valentin Haüy.

It had been at the Royal Court of Versailles during the Christmas celebrations in 1786. Haüy had astonished the king and queen and a large audience of the nobility of France with a unique display of blind children reading and doing arithmetic!

Indeed the marquis himself was much impressed. He joined the royal couple and many others in donating money to Haüy's new school for blind girls and boys.

Urged on by the determined Palluy, the marquis wrote at once to the director of the school in Paris and asked him to allow Louis to become a pupil.

A reply came quickly. Dr. Sebastien Guillié, director of the Royal Institution for Blind Children, informed the marquis that the directors of the institution in Paris had agreed to offer Louis a place. They even offered him a small scholarship to help pay school tuition.

They expected Louis to join the institution on February 15, 1819, at its building on the street named Rue Saint-Victor. He would start school shortly after his tenth birthday.

The journey to Paris

The long-awaited day dawned misty and cold. The stagecoach from the nearby town of Meaux was to carry ten-year-old Louis twenty-five miles (40 km) through the winter landscape to Paris.

He had looked forward to this day. Yet now that it was here, he was chattering in a confusion of excitement and nervousness, soaring hopes and plunging anxieties.

Would it be as he wanted it to be? So far away! Would he be able to learn? Would he make new friends? Would it be difficult to find his way around?

His father was also talking a lot, describing the scenes passing by outside the coach so that Louis could share them. Simon-René too was deeply worried. He kept telling himself that it must be for the best to have his son go somewhere where he could learn things.

But it seemed so far from his village home. He was still so young. Yet, Simon-René thought, if Louis could at least learn a skill. The school taught several trades — slippermaking, shoemaking, basketry, knitting, spinning and weaving, ropemaking, and chairmending, among others.

But what a gigantic city to leave him alone in! Even he, the adult and sighted Simon-René, found Paris strange and frightening. It was so large, so noisy, and so full of strangers. It was all so different from the unhurried life of Coupvray.

Four hours of jolting and rumbling and worrying and wondering went by. Louis and his father came to the edge of Paris and climbed down from the coach. From here on, they would have to find their way on

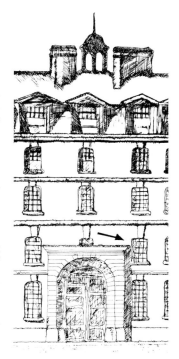

The Royal Institution for Blind Children. The school changed rapidly during the stormy years of the French Revolution and the years following. Haüy's reputation also rose and fell with the political changes sweeping the country.

foot to the bustling Latin Quarter, an area on the Left Bank of the Seine River famous for its schools and student life.

Somewhere close by was the street Rue Saint-Victor and number 68. Although Louis and his father did not know it, this building was to become Louis' home for the rest of his life.

68 Rue Saint-Victor

It was not an attractive sight, that building on Rue Saint-Victor. Official reports of the time tell us that the house was "in a low-lying district which is airless, evil-smelling and conducive to the spread of disease."

It was dark and damp, a maze of worn stairways and cramped corridors that must have filled Simon-René with unease. Where was the clear air of

In 1819, Louis' short journey to Paris took four hours by stagecoach. Although he had often listened in Coupvray to the stagecoach driver give news of Paris and the countryside, this was his first ride in a stagecoach.

Coupvray? Where was the energetic outdoor life that Louis was used to leading with his friends and family in the countryside?

But the meeting with the director, Dr. Guillié, set his father's mind at rest. The staff and pupils would take good care of the boy, and there was a great deal he would learn here. In no time, he would be back for his summer vacation. And Louis, although nervous, was so insistent that this was what he really wanted.

A brief, close hug, many reassurances, and Simon-René left. Now Louis was truly alone. In a building he did not know, strangers he could not see surrounded him for the first time in his life.

Unfamiliar surroundings

The director took him straight to a class taught by Monsieur P. Armand Dufau. Nervously, Louis entered. The sound of shuffling feet told him that the pupils had risen to their feet. There was a rustling as they turned to the door, then an abrupt order from Guillié that they should concentrate on their lessons.

Louis felt himself led by the teacher to a seat, and without further fuss, the class was resumed. It was a geography lesson about the route of the great Seine River through France.

But soon, his nervousness, anxiety, and shyness had flown. Louis knew nothing anymore but his teacher's words. He absorbed every syllable with a fascinated attention. Much to the teacher's surprise, at the end of the lesson, he could answer all of the teacher's questions without hesitating.

But after the lesson, the feeling of strangeness swooped in on him again. What did the ringing bells mean? Where were all the feet going? The teacher introduced him to the other pupils, and he tried to memorize their names and their voices. But it was all just a mass of new smells, more bells, and hurrying feet that seemed to know exactly where they were going. He stood, miserably confused, until someone took his arm and led him on.

Later, after he had unpacked his few belongings and put them beneath his bed, there was the silence of the dormitory and the awareness of other, unseen strangers in their iron beds just like his.

"When he [Louis Braille] first came to the house, a certain childish gravity was remarkable in him, and this was well suited to the delicacy of his features and the gentleness and intelligence of his expression."
Dr. André Pignier,
Biographical Notes on Three Former Professors of the Institution for Blind Children

"There were sixty pupils, and the headmaster treated them with great severity, punishing the boys for the most trivial offences by depriving them of their meals or sending them into solitary confinement."
Norman Wymer,
The Inventors

23

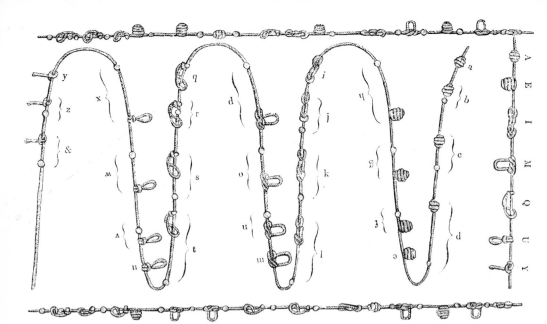

Over the centuries, people in different countries had tried to find ways of communicating the alphabet to blind people. Using the unique method pictured above, blind people could read letters by feeling the pattern of the knots in the string.

New horizons

But at some stage in those first few days, he made a friend, Gabriel Gauthier. He was to remain Louis' closest friend for the rest of his life. Gauthier had been at the school for some time, although he was only a year older than Louis.

Gauthier knew his way around the endless corridors and twisting stairs and understood the routine of life here. In his company, Louis slowly learned too, as they moved from lesson to lesson, from room to room, and from meal to dormitory.

There were also letters from his family in Coupvray to help him through the early weeks. One of the supervisors at the school read his letters to him. The sense of newness faded and the surroundings became familiar, part of his own territory.

Now he could find his own way around the confusing hallways and schoolrooms. He knew without counting when he had moved enough steps along the corridor to the stairs. He knew how far it was from the dormitory door to his bed, from the classrooms to the courtyard and to the dining room. He learned to recognize the voices of the boys and teachers around him.

And above all there were the lessons. Geography, history, arithmetic, and grammar — he plunged into them with enthusiasm, showing all the promise that Palluy had been certain was there. These lessons tested Louis' ability to memorize what he heard.

The teachers spoke to the pupils, and the pupils repeated what they heard. And wonder of wonders, there were even some books and pamphlets prepared especially for blind students. Louis was actually learning to read!

Haüy's books for blind people

Haüy, founder of the school, had developed a way of printing books for blind people. Heavy paper was pressed onto a special, large lead type to make embossed letters raised above the surface of the page that could be felt by the fingers.

There weren't many of these books in the school because it was slow work and they were difficult to make. Each letter had to be individually put in position and each piece of dampened paper put in the press and imprinted. It took weeks to make several copies of a single page. So it was not surprising that over the years, Haüy had succeeded in producing only a handful of books and pamphlets.

The books were big and clumsy. Each page consisted of two pieces of paper pasted together so that the raised letters on each side faced outward. There were several religious texts and some grammar books in different languages. It was a strange collection to make up the basic library of the sixty or so children who were the pupils at the institution. But still, they were books!

After being excited when he first felt those raised letters under his fingers, Louis had to admit that he was increasingly frustrated. Reading was so slow. Each letter had to be traced with your fingertips. Then you had to remember it while you went on to the next one. You had to remember all the letters in the correct order until your fingers had passed the length of the whole word. It was easy to forget the first letters by the time you reached the end. And although Louis made good progress, it was difficult to feel the forms of the letters.

Valentin Haüy's embossed books for blind people were as large as the book pictured above. A print book transcribed into Haüy's system was bulky and required several volumes.

A talented pupil

But Louis' craft lessons posed no problems — basketry, knitting, slippermaking, he enjoyed them all. Showing again the dexterity and accuracy of his fingers that his family had discovered in his tasks at home, he won prizes in knitting and slippermaking at the end of his first school year.

And there was music! Teachers came especially from the Paris Conservatory of Music to the school to teach students the flute, the bassoon, and the piano. They taught by guiding the pupils' hands along the instrument until they had memorized the position of the notes and the sounds they should make.

From the beginning, Louis discovered a special pleasure in playing music. He learned to play the piano. It quickly gave him a sense of freedom that flowed through his playing and marked him as a skillful player whose natural talent would grow.

A new director

Near the beginning of Louis' third year at the school, in 1821, there was an important change. Guillié, the director, was dismissed and a new director appointed. The pupils knew nothing about the reasons for Guillié's removal, but they were not sorry to see him go. For all his work at the school, he had been an abrupt, aloof man. He had run the school strictly, with many harsh rules.

The new director, André Pignier, was very different. He seems to have been a dedicated man with a strong interest in the progress of the pupils in his care at the institution.

We also know a great deal more about Louis because of Dr. Pignier. He has left behind his own written memories of the young student from his first meetings with Louis.

There was also much excitement in those early months of 1821. The school was preparing to welcome its founder, Valentin Haüy.

The old man had not visited the school for many years. The government of France had changed rapidly during the first few years of the school and had not approved of several of Haüy's actions. So he had accepted Czar Alexander I's invitation to go to

Braille's love of music and skill at playing the organ and piano might have provided one possible future for him if he had not invented his system. At least his parents could now hope that he could earn money as a musician — as the blind bagpipe player is in this painting.

Russia to organize a project for educating blind children there. He had just returned to Paris in 1817 after eleven years away. Efforts to revisit the school he had worked so hard to organize had saddened him. Guillié had not welcomed him at all. But the new director and the rest of the staff at the institution were eager to honor the man who had struggled for seventeen years to establish the first school for blind children in the world.

But Haüy had done much more than simply offer education to the uneducated. He promoted the idea that blind people were equal to all other people and should have the same opportunities in life, such as a chance to be educated and independent. And his idea had gained support. In Germany, Austria, Prussia, England, and Russia, schools for blind children had begun, inspired by the one in Paris.

"What the blind so passionately desire and expect from us is that we should draw them into the great family circle of mankind where they will be but one link in the same human chain, ordinary men and women."

Jean Roblin,
Louis Braille

The founder's legacy

Haüy himself had understood how big the gap was between sighted people and blind people only when he had witnessed a group of blind musicians performing as clowns. Costumed in donkeys' ears attached to dunce caps and wearing huge cardboard glasses, they sawed tunelessly on old musical instruments in front of sheets of music turned the wrong way. The crowd hooted at this spectacle at the September 1771 fair of St. Ovid.

The experience had shocked the twenty-six-year-old Haüy to the core. He decided that he would substitute the truth for this mocking parody. He would put books into the hands of blind people, books that they had printed.

But what prejudices he had to overcome in other people before they took him seriously! For centuries, sighted people had responded to blind people with pity, derision, or actual cruelty. The belief that blind people must be stupid was deep-rooted. People were not easily convinced that there was much point in spending time or money on trying to teach blind people thought to be unable to learn.

It had been difficult to find both money for his venture and blind people who would agree to be taught. In 1784, he had taken his first pupil off the streets, thirteen years after the fair. This seventeen-year-old beggar named François Lesueur had daily haunted the porch of the Church of St. Germain.

Lesueur had been blind since he was six weeks old. As long as he could remember, he had been begging for his living. Haüy offered him a home and his first lessons. He also promised him wages equal to the money he made by begging.

He started teaching Lesueur to read with movable wooden letters carved on thin tablets that he arranged to form words. It worked — Lesueur could read!

Haüy also found that Lesueur could recognize the imprint of letters on the reverse side of a page. Inspired by the idea of raised print, Haüy embossed several pages. With some pride, he was able to show his pupil's skill to the Royal Academy, the assembly of France's foremost scholars and scientists. Lesueur's proficiency at reading caused a sensation.

The fair at St. Ovid in 1771, where Valentin Haüy saw blind people clowning to the shouts and jeers of the audience. In earlier times, blind people had been considered useless and were killed at birth or abandoned to die when they grew old.

A school for blind children

Haüy's dream had become a reality. The world had its first school for blind children, twenty-four pupils gathered in an old house in Paris. Then came the display at the Court of Versailles that the Marquis d'Orvilliers had witnessed. More donations had allowed the school to grow. In 1791, the government finally made the school a state institution.

But in the end, state control had also led to the school's merging, at Napoleon's orders, with a refuge for elderly blind people called the Hospital of Quinze-Vingts.* A year later, Haüy was fired.

Now no longer a hospital and shelter, the institution had regained its independence and was once more a real school for children. But the aged founder had never been allowed to visit the institution he had fought so hard to create. Now one of the first acts of the new director was to remedy this.

Haüy visits the school

At once, Pignier formally invited Haüy, now an old man in his seventies, to pay an official visit to the institution. They would not skimp on their efforts to please him — decorations in the classrooms, displays of learning and crafts, followed by a musical party. It would be the highlight of the term.

Louis remembered that meeting with the old man all his life. Instantly, he sensed the great happiness flowing from this brave pioneer as he saw, at last, the evidence of his work. The children here were living proof of his efforts. They played music, recited poetry, and sang a song dedicated to him as thanks for opening a world to them that was denied to so many other blind people.

How different these children were from the blind beggars and the costumed blind musicians exhibited at fairs who had first aroused Haüy's sympathy!

---

*The French term *Quinze-Vingts* literally means "fifteen twenties" (15 x 20) and refers to the three hundred blind people for whom the hospital was originally founded.

This statue of Valentin Haüy with François Lesueur now stands in the grounds of the modern National Institution for Blind Children in Paris. It commemorates that first act of compassion and imagination by Valentin Haüy, when he took Lesueur as his first pupil and taught him to read.

A text printed in the large embossed letters developed by Valentin Haüy. These books were large and heavy — some subjects needed as many as twenty volumes, each weighing about twenty pounds (9 kg).

Along with the other students, Louis sang and shook hands with Haüy. New seeds of conviction and determination were sown in young Louis that day. For these last few months had brought another discovery to Louis that had fired his mind with fresh excitement and new ambitions.

Barbier's dots and dashes

Charles Barbier, an artillery captain in King Louis XVIII's army, came to Pignier with an interesting proposal. He had invented a form of writing using only raised dots and dashes. He had developed it so that military orders could be passed between soldiers secretly at night, no matter how dark it was. He had called the system "night writing."

But then he had seen a display at the Museum of Industry. Blind pupils had been demonstrating their reading from Haüy's books, those large pages filled with big embossed letters. Captain Barbier had been struck by how slowly the children had to trace each letter's outline.

It had prompted him to do further work, changing his night writing so that it could be used by blind people. He had explained the system, which he had renamed sonography, to Pignier. It did not use individual letters to spell out the words but expressed whole sounds by groups of dots and dashes.

Over the years, there had been several inventors knocking at the door of the institution. But once tried by the pupils, their ideas had proved useless.

Admittedly, the use of dots was something new. Other systems had all been based on the alphabet used by sighted people, changed so that it could be felt instead of seen.

This suggestion about dots and dashes was different enough for Pignier to listen carefully and discuss the invention in some detail. Captain Barbier had to smother his impatience and be content with waiting for a while because the director insisted that the system be tried out by the blind pupils.

Louis and his friends first knew of the captain's invention when Pignier called the whole school together a few days later. There was a good deal of talk about the meeting. What could be so important as to gather them all together? Sixty children shuffled anxiously amid equally intrigued supervisors and teachers. They expected some new changes to the school organization or staffing. But they were unprepared for the long and careful description of Captain Barbier's invention and for the few embossed pages that Pignier passed around for them to feel.

Louis masters the system

Dots! Louis was transfixed. One can imagine the students' slowly tracing the dots, murmurs of interest rippling among them. They explored the different shapes, slowly becoming more excited as they all realized how easy it was to tell these shapes apart. Much easier than those large embossed letters in the books they were used to!

There were excited cries. Everyone had an opinion. Some children felt intimidated by the idea of learning something new because it was slightly complicated. It was faster, felt others. And with this system, the students realized they could write, too.

"Like so many of the inventions that have been blessings to mankind, it came about accidentally. Opening up the world of written language to the blind was the furthest thing from the mind of the man [Charles Barbier] who devised the basic concept that made it possible."

Frances A. Koestler,
The Unseen Minority: A
Social History of
Blindness in the
United States

All agreed that the students would try the new system. So the director informed Barbier that his sonography would be added as an "auxiliary method of teaching."

Louis and his fellow pupils were eager to learn the new writing system. With Louis' quick intelligence and nimble fingers, he quickly grasped the process of making words out of sounds expressed in dots. He learned Barbier's chart containing all the combinations of dots and dashes and became skilled with the device that Barbier had developed for writing with his system.

This equipment was simple but clever. There was a ruler with seven shallow grooves on it that stretched over its full length. To write, you placed the paper on this ruler. A clip fit over the paper and slid along the ruler. In the sliding clip were little windows through which the writer could place the dots precisely on the paper, locating them neatly in the ruler's grooves.

Dots or dashes were made with the aid of a stylus, a slim, pointed instrument with a large, round handle. You simply punched it down, pressing dots into heavy paper so that on the reverse side they could be felt as bumps. The writer moved from right to left along the paper so that when it was turned over, the words could be read from left to right.

Throughout that winter, the pupils worked with enthusiasm using Barbier's invention. They were fascinated by the idea of being able to write, of being able to do some real reading. Braille and Gauthier spent many extra hours writing sentences to each other and then reading them back.

Problems with Barbier's system

But the better Louis became at using sonography, the more he had to admit there were problems with it. For a start, you couldn't spell with it — it was only designed to represent words as a collection of sounds. You couldn't put commas or periods or any kind of punctuation in your sentences because Barbier had not worked out any combination of dots for that. Nor could you put any accent on a word, which is an essential part of spelling in French, or write numbers or do mathematics or write music.

And there were so many dots for a single word! Each symbol might be as many as six dots deep. A single syllable of a word might need as many as twenty dots! There were too many dots for the students to feel with one finger, and it was so hard to remember all the symbols. Writing using Barbier's system was difficult too. There were so many dots to punch and the dashes were difficult to make.

Without doubt, it was better than the embossed letters of Haüy. But gradually they all agreed that there were too many dots in each word, and the dots didn't say enough.

Louis meets Captain Barbier

Louis tried to improve Barbier's system. His experiments seemed to work. Excitedly, he showed them to Pignier. The director, rather impressed, suggested that he should talk to Barbier. The inventor, equally intrigued, visited the school again to discuss Louis' ideas.

The precise details of the meeting between Louis and Barbier have not been recorded. But we do know that Barbier was startled to find that a boy of thirteen claimed to have solved problems with his system that he had failed to solve.

While Barbier agreed that many of Louis' small improvements were useful, he disagreed with Louis about whether his system needed basic changes. But Louis was convinced that the number of dots should be reduced and that spelling and punctuation should be added.

For all his concern for the blind children to whom he had offered sonography, the captain could not share Louis' belief that they needed an elaborate system such as the one Louis envisioned. What could blind people want other than a basic way to communicate? Why should they want the full alphabet, punctuation, and even mathematics and music that this ambitious boy was suggesting?

He did not understand their desire for something that would allow blind people to enter the world of literature and science fully, able to read and compose the most complex thoughts and convey them to others on paper.

B	D	G
J	V	Z
R	GN	LL
IEN	ION	IEU

Barbier's sonography. The dots refer to a grid of six lines across by six rows down, in which Barbier placed sounds. The dots indicated the position of each sound in this grid. You counted the number of dots in the first column to find out which row down, then those in the second column to find out which line across.

Louis experiments

Faced with the stubborn Barbier, who insisted that his system was as good as it needed to be, Louis gave up trying to convince him. But he was certain that he could improve the system. With or without Barbier, he would experiment and simplify. He would find something that was right, that was easy to learn and do. He would devise a system that could do everything a writing and reading language should do, with all the flexibility of the regular alphabet.

And so thirteen-year-old Louis set off on his quest. He worked in all the spare moments he could snatch from his busy day of lessons. He took up his task again at night as soon as the dormitory fell quiet and resumed it in the early hours of the morning. He pored over it on his long summer vacation in Coupvray, calculating, experimenting, revising, working on and on.

First, he had to reduce the number of dots so that each symbol could be instantly felt beneath one fingertip. He also had to remove any arrangement of dots or dashes that might be confused with another arrangement. Each group of dots had to be obviously different from any other. There was a solution. He was certain. It was only a question of finding it.

The dawn of braille

By October 1824, when the new school year began, Louis felt his alphabet was ready. He had found a way of forming all the letters, accents, punctuation marks, and mathematical signs using just six dots and some small dashes. The cluster of dots for each sign was now so small that there was no need to move your finger — you could feel the whole group at once.

When Louis' friend Gauthier heard, he could not contain his excitement. Groups of pupils gathered around as Louis wrote with dazzling speed and accuracy. Within hours, the whole school knew, and Louis was called to show Pignier what he had done. The director was fascinated as he watched Louis rapidly demonstrate his idea — it was so simple, so accurate, and so clear. Just six dots. But the brilliant child had found a way of forming them into sixty-three combinations. This idea could work!

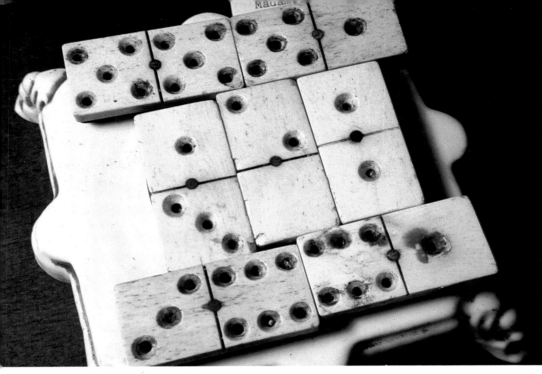

Above: Braille's personal dominoes. The dots were removed to leave small dents that he could feel with his fingers.

Left: A Barbier ruler for writing adapted for Louis' six-dot system is shown on the left. On the right is an original Barbier ruler. The rulers are lying on an early version of Braille's alphabet, one that still included the dashes he later removed.

35

There were still some details to solve, Louis assured him earnestly. Without hesitating, the director congratulated the young pupil and urged him to continue his experiments.

It took the other students little time to learn Louis' system. It held none of the problems they had experienced with Barbier's dots. Impressed with their enthusiasm for it and the speed of their progress, Pignier had Barbier's rulers adapted for Louis' dots. The large windows in the sliding clip were divided into two smaller ones so that each window allowed a maximum of six dots to be positioned within it.

For the first time, the pupils could take notes, write letters to each other, keep diaries, write stories, and copy passages or even whole books they liked. Finally, they could do all those things that a sighted person takes for granted and that had been out of reach until now.

For blind people, it was the dawn of a new age.

Teacher and musician

His friends' excitement and enthusiasm were proof for Braille that his system worked. He continued experimenting and perfecting his "little system," as he called it. But he never neglected his other activities. His life was still full, despite all this work on his system. He continued to excel in his studies.

In 1826, still only a student of seventeen, Braille began to teach algebra, grammar, and geography to the younger pupils. He had found his vocation — this blind student was quickly becoming an excellent teacher of blind children. With his gentle manner, lively gestures, quick intelligence, and liking and concern for his students, he was perfectly suited to his new profession.

Music continued to give Braille great pleasure. By now he was studying the organ. In later years, he became the organist at several churches in the city. This position combined for Braille the chance to play the music he loved and the freedom to express his deep religious faith. Braille's friend and pupil, Hippolyte Coltat, tells us that his playing of the organ was "correct, brilliant, easy, typical of the whole tone of his personality."

Below: St. Nicholas du Chardonnet, a nearby church that students from the institution attended. Holding on to a length of rope as a guide, they would make their way to Mass through the narrow streets of Paris.

The evolution of braille

We can trace the development and perfection of Braille's "little system" over subsequent years. First, in 1827, he made a version of a grammar book using his dot alphabet. Two years later he made a version of another grammar text.

In 1828, he extended his system to the copying of music. By now he had removed the dashes from his alphabet. Practice had shown that although they were easy to feel, the dashes were difficult to write well with the stylus.

By 1829, Braille published the first edition of his *Method of Writing Words, Music and Plain Songs by Means of Dots, for Use by the Blind and Arranged for Them.* This book was the formal birth of the original braille alphabet. But it would be many more years before it was officially adopted, even in Braille's own institution. And even some teachers there continued to object to the use of this system by students.

In his opening to this book, Braille compared the improvements in his system with the system developed by Barbier. Yet he was totally honest in giving Barbier full credit for the style of writing by dots. "We must say," he wrote, "that his method gave us the first idea of our own."

"He never lost sight of this work. Never for an instant did he shirk the task of refining, developing and practicing his new way of writing and reading."
Hippolyte Coltat,
Louis Braille's friend

Below, left: The embossed music produced by Valentin Haüy. It had all the drawbacks of the large embossed letters.

Below, right: Braille music of 1841. With this system, blind musicians could not only read music but also compose their own.

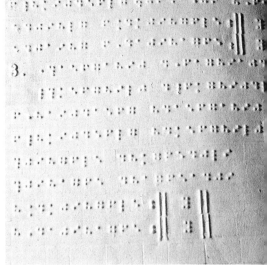

An inspired teacher

In August 1828, at the age of nineteen, Louis Braille officially became a teacher at the Royal Institution for Blind Children. When school began again after summer vacation, he started teaching grammar, geography, arithmetic, and music.

As a teacher, Braille inspired his students constantly. Since he remembered his early struggles as a student there, he knew how to explain subjects so that his students understood their lessons.

"He carried out his duties with so much charm and wisdom," wrote Coltat, "that the obligation of attending his class was transformed into a real pleasure for his pupils. They competed not only to equal and surpass each other, but also in a touching and constant effort to please a teacher whom they admired as a superior and liked as a wise and well-informed friend, ready with sound advice."

Life continued for Louis the teacher in much the same way as it had for Louis the pupil. He wore the same kind of uniform he had as a student with the addition of silk and gold braid to mark his new status. The rules for students and teachers seem very harsh at this distance of over 150 years. He was unable to leave the school without permission and his letters were read before being passed on to him. And this was under the easy rule of Pignier!

But he no longer had to sleep in the dormitory. He had a room to himself. It was strange, at first, not to sense the others sleeping all around him. But then what a luxury it was to have the peace and quiet to concentrate on his studies and research when the day's activities were over.

Braille prepared his lessons using his own alphabet and began work on a book on arithmetic. His research on writing music progressed.

Braille was happy. His teaching absorbed him, his research absorbed him, and his friends absorbed him. Coltat and Gauthier had also been made apprentice teachers. They would sit in Braille's room and discuss what was happening at the school and in France. Often Pignier would invite them to his home and to social events so they would have some social life outside the school.

Opposite: A teacher guides the hands of a blind child along a piano keyboard. In the past, many blind people have earned their living as singers, pianists, organists, and violinists. Most traditional schools for blind children strongly stressed musical skills.

"With him [Louis Braille] friendship was a conscientious duty as well as a tender sentiment. He would have sacrificed everything to it — his time, his health and his possessions."

Hippolyte Coltat, Louis Braille's friend

A time of loss

But the year 1831 brought bad news. His brother Louis-Simon arrived to tell him that their father had died. To his end, Simon-René had worried about the fate of his blind son, still only twenty-two years old. Louis-Simon brought with him their father's last letter, dictated on his deathbed and addressed to Pignier. In it, Simon-René asked the director never to abandon Louis, never to turn him out.

That evening Braille left for Coupvray to be with his family in this time of grief and to help his mother through the early days of loss. At least he was fulfilling his father's dearest wish — he had a profession and an income of his own. He could be a comfort to his mother and he would not be a burden, as so many blind people were.

Failing health

In these early years of the 1830s, Braille was often sick. By 1835, he could not ignore the increasing signs of some deep-seated illness. He was only in his mid-twenties, but he was always tired, frequently seized by fevers and often troubled by a tightness in his chest.

One night, he awoke burning with fever, his mouth filling suddenly with blood. Desperately, he called for help.

The school doctor easily diagnosed what was wrong. Braille had suffered a sudden attack of internal bleeding. There could be no doubt that the young man was in the first stages of tuberculosis, a lung disease for which there was no cure.

At that time, doctors knew little about tuberculosis except to recognize the symptoms of coughing, fatigue, and fever. They did not yet know that it was caused by a germ. The close, damp air of places like the school and its dirty, crowded neighborhood in Paris made it easy for this germ to be carried from one person to another. Clean, fresh air might have helped, but the only prescription the doctor could give was to rest more and eat well.

At once, Pignier arranged the teaching duties of his staff so that Braille had only small classes. He would have to talk far less and prepare little.

Forced to reduce his teaching duties, Braille continued instead with his research. In 1836, he added the letter *W* to his alphabet at the request of an English pupil at the school. This was necessary because the letter *W* does not appear in French.

A year later, he published a revised edition of the book on his system. He continued to call it his "little system of writing by means of dots" — unaware that his name would one day be immortalized, when the "little system" became known worldwide as braille.

Raphigraphy

Now Braille became interested in how blind people and sighted people could write to each other. His raised dots were of no use for this because they relied on the sighted person's learning braille. What was needed was a way for blind people to write that sighted people could read without special training. He thought he could find a way.

By 1839, Braille had a solution. He developed a way of using the forms of the ordinary letters of the alphabet, maps, geometric figures, and music. But he made these forms out of raised dots. Blind people could feel them, and sighted people could instantly see them!

Braille called this invention raphigraphy, and the students at the institution seized on it as eagerly as they had taken up his six-dot alphabet. Now they could write to their parents and know their letters could be read.

François-Pierre Foucault, a creative and blind friend of Braille who lived at the Hospital of Quinze-Vingts, increased the usefulness of this invention. He developed a machine for printing raphigraphy. He attached type to levers that were struck to imprint the letters on paper. It was no less than an early ancestor of the typewriter!

The more Braille worked on his research, the more he perfected an extraordinary precision with words. So much space was needed to convey any word for blind people, even in his own system! The utmost economy was needed. And Braille was a genius at precision — this is why braille was to become the best system for blind people.

Louis Braille's raphigraphy, a method of representing the letters of the ordinary alphabet with raised dots.

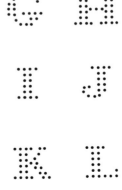

Above: A braille globe of the world. Braille can be applied to any device requiring the use of the alphabet, numbers, music, or scientific symbols.

Opposition

Since 1829, Pignier had repeatedly asked that Braille's system be recognized as the official one at the school. In 1834, he had even arranged for Braille to demonstrate braille at the Exhibition of Industry held at the Place de La Concorde, the great square in Paris. And in 1837, the printing press of the institution produced a three-volume history of France — the first book ever to be printed in braille.

But Pignier's requests for braille to be fully recognized were not granted by the governing body of the school. Officially, the school still had to use Haüy's embossed letters, although they were bulky, ill-suited, and useful only in printed form. Attempts over the years to teach blind people to write these letters had not succeeded.

But to change the system would be expensive. The books would have to be reprinted, the instruments replaced, and all the teaching methods changed.

There were also many people who believed that the system used by blind people must be one based on the same principles as the alphabet used by sighted people. To involve blind people in a special alphabet, so the argument went, would create a strong barrier between blind people and sighted people. This idea would persist in different forms for many decades. It was a major stumbling block for other countries trying to declare braille the official alphabet for their blind citizens.

Braille was disappointed by the lack of support from the authorities and even wrote to the Ministry of the Interior himself. He received no reply. It was not until 1840, sixteen years after he had first devised braille, that the first ray of hope was sent out from the officials. In reply to another of Pignier's renewed requests, the answer this time was only, "This work strikes me as remarkable, and I think that Monsieur Braille ought to be encouraged." For all Braille's efforts, it was still Haüy's method that had to be taught officially to the children at the institution.

Pignier is forced out

Braille was severely disappointed in several ways that year. For some time, Dufau, the vice principal of the school, had been trying to get rid of Pignier and gain control of the school himself. Because of the times, this was not difficult for Dufau.

Over the past few decades, the government of France had been changing rapidly. King Louis XVIII's brother, Charles X, succeeded him in 1824 and became king. Gradually, Charles reduced the power of the representatives that the people of France had elected. In time, the French people revolted, and in 1830, he was forced to abdicate. Charles X's cousin, Louis Philippe, became king and the parliament approved a constitution.

But liberal and conservative factions continued to argue for different systems of government. All these shifts in government and the general unrest of the era made life uncertain for people such as Pignier whose jobs were controlled by the government. In 1840, with the help of one of the other teachers, Dufau finally succeeded in his plan. He persuaded the authorities that Pignier's teaching of history corrupted the pupils' minds. The authorities forced Pignier to retire early and appointed Dufau in his place as director.

The school had lost the man who had for twenty years devoted himself to the education and care of blind children. And they had lost their main champion of braille. Pignier had always allowed them to use it in the school, even though it was not officially recognized. From now on, it would be a very different matter. Dufau was not renowned for his support of braille. Braille and the pupils feared problems in trying to continue with it.

A bust of Louis Braille. His friend Hippolyte Coltat described Braille as having blond, curly hair. He was relaxed in his manner yet purposeful and agile in his movement. But the pallor of his face warned of his frail health.

The new principal

The years of 1840 and 1841 were unhappy for Braille. In June 1841, his second sister, Marie-Céline, died in Coupvray. She was only forty-three and she left behind two young children, ages six and thirteen. The family's worry about Braille made their sense of loss worse. He was constantly ill.

And the school under Dufau was not pleasant. He wanted to establish his authority as director without question. He seemed to want to change everything. Each day brought something new, introduced at great speed. He paid little attention to how distressing the pupils might find the rapid transformation from the way the school used to be. And unlike Pignier, he punished the students severely for breaking the rules of the institution.

Dufau was also one of those who believed firmly that blind people should use the same alphabet as sighted people did. Using a special one would separate them, he argued, and close them off from normal intellectual life. He held firmly to these views despite the obvious fact that the students clearly preferred braille over the embossed alphabet.

Braille's health worsens

Braille's health was declining. He lost even more weight. And in the first months of 1843, he had more internal bleeding and began to cough blood again. He was forced to take to his bed for weeks at a time.

Dr. Allibert, the school's doctor, was insistent that he needed far more rest and that he must give up his teaching. Braille and Dufau agreed.

The weeks went by. Visits from Braille's friends kept him current on even the smallest incidents in the school. Warmer weather seemed to bring an improvement in his health. He began going out with Gauthier and Coltat to visit Pignier, who lived nearby since his forced retirement from the school. They would visit the botanical gardens or stop at the park to hear the ducks quacking.

But on his return from one of these walks, Braille suffered further heavy internal bleeding. Allibert feared the worst. He insisted that Braille go home to the country to rest.

"Once he [Louis Braille] had resolved to do something he would carry it through conscientiously. It did not matter whether the task was pleasant or unpleasant, but only whether it was useful."
Hippolyte Coltat,
Louis Braille's friend

A painting by the famous French artist Jean Baptiste Camille Corot of a typical country village during Braille's lifetime.

Home to Coupvray

Braille stayed in Coupvray for six months. Being home seemed to help. Gone were all the difficulties of being at school, such as the worries and the unpleasant atmosphere of rivalry and intrigue caused by Dufau. Fresh air and his mother's cooking and care also helped. He began to feel better.

Yet Coupvray, too, held some sorrow for Braille that year of 1843. Antoine Bécheret died. He was the last of that trio of people who had been so important in Braille's early life — the Abbé Palluy and the Marquis d'Orvilliers were already dead.

But Braille was pleased to be with the younger members of the family, his sisters' children. He was particularly close to his eight-year-old niece, Céline-Louise, his dead sister's youngest daughter. He spent long hours walking and talking with her.

Back to Paris

In October 1843, a refreshed Braille returned to Paris. But he found that conditions were a lot worse at school. The example of teachers of blind people in Scotland and the United States had influenced Dufau. He was changing the size of Haüy's embossed letters and had burned all the old books printed in the original embossed alphabet!

All twenty-six printed by Guillié and the forty-seven printed by Pignier had gone up in flames and smoke. Now the blind pupils would have to learn to read all over again, getting used to completely new sizes and shapes! Braille's dot alphabet was, needless to say, not included in Dufau's teaching plans, except for writing music.

But the pupils clung obstinately to braille. They taught each other outside the official classes and used

The Braille family house in Coupvray as it is now. Since the one-hundredth anniversary of Louis Braille's death, the house and his father's workshop have been preserved as a museum.

it for all their own notes and letters, refusing to let go. Realizing the strength of their attachment, Dufau now openly opposed it, forbidding them to use it.

Help came unexpectedly, from a friend of Dufau himself — Joseph Gaudet, his own new deputy. Gaudet could not ignore the evidence of his eyes. The blind pupils insisted Braille's system was better than anything else. And how fast they could work with it! By comparison, the progress made with Haüy's letters, even in the new sizes, was pitifully slow.

Gaudet resolved to persuade the obstinate Dufau of the system's merits. More books could be transcribed into braille than could be made with Haüy's embossed letters. It would not isolate blind people. What better access to science, the arts, and to education itself than more books for them to read?

Blind guests arriving for a social gathering. Compare this situation to the one depicted in the painting by Brueghel on page 18 that also shows "the blind leading the blind."

A new school

Among the stream of famous visitors who had visited the famous school was a well-known poet and historian named Alphonse Marie Louis de Lamartine. He had entered politics and had become a deputy in the Chamber of Deputies. In 1838, he had spoken with conviction about the appalling living conditions on Rue Saint-Victor. The Chamber of Deputies had been deeply moved by his description. They had swiftly voted enough money to buy some land on the Boulevard des Invalides, near the armed forces hospital, and to build a new school there.

By November of 1843, the new building was ready. It must have been with a strange mixture of emotions that the pupils of Rue Saint-Victor packed up and moved. The unsanitary old building had been home to many of them for years. But how spacious, clean, and airy the new buildings were! And perhaps Louis Braille would never have contracted tuberculosis had he spent his life in such uncrowded, healthful surroundings.

"Yesterday I visited the Royal Institution for Blind Children. No description could give you a true idea of this building, which is small, dirty and gloomy; of those passages partitioned off to form boxes dignified by the name of workshops or classrooms, of those many tortuous, worm-eaten staircases, which, far from seeming suited to unfortunates who can guide themselves only by their sense of touch, are . . . more like a challenge flung down to these children's blindness."
Alphonse de Lamartine in his speech to France's Chamber of Deputies

Approval for Braille's system

The new school at 56 Boulevard des Invalides officially opened on February 22, 1844. A large and distinguished audience, including members of the French government and the students' relatives and friends, gathered for the ceremony. They were unaware that they were about to witness another momentous event. The school choir sang a song composed by Dufau and Gauthier as a tribute to Haüy. Pupils recited poetry and played music. Then it was Gaudet's turn to make a speech.

To Braille's amazement, it was announced that Dufau was going to describe the system of writing in raised dots! The director proceeded to tell the audience about the problems with Barbier's sonography and then the enormous advantages of Braille's system. He paid full tribute to the young inventor seated among them. In no uncertain terms, Dufau had forced the public to hear about braille. An announcement to such a gathering, accompanied by a pamphlet on the subject, meant that the school had finally approved the forbidden dots!

In 1843, the Royal Institution for Blind Children moved to new buildings in a lighter, cleaner, airier part of Paris on the Boulevard des Invalides. The armed forces hospital, called Les Invalides, and the elegant gardens shown in this picture are at the northern end of this wide boulevard.

The blind pupils' persistence and devotion to the system of dots had triumphed. After twenty years of determination, Louis Braille's tremendous invention was officially acknowledged.

When the speech was over, Gaudet supervised a few experiments before the intrigued audience. One of the blind girls wrote down some poetry dictated by a member of the audience. Another girl, who had not been in the room during the dictation, now entered and proceeded to read the writing perfectly. Then Gaudet had one of the teachers write down a musical phrase, dictated by one of the audience. Another blind pupil entered the room and played it back, again perfectly. And all so fast, so easily executed.

There was thunderous applause. Braille was thrilled. Surely the continual battle for his system to be adopted was over.

Dufau makes amends

It certainly seems that Dufau had been completely won over. In the following years, he seems to have tried to make amends for his earlier behavior. As Braille grew sicker, Dufau worked hard for permission to care for him at the institution.

For in spite of being happy about the opening ceremony, Braille was feeling ill again. Fatigue, excitement about the move, and teaching his classes combined to place heavy demands on his already frail health. His cough worsened and he tired easily. Within months, Dufau relieved him of all duties and asked to keep Braille at the institution to give him the care he needed.

Braille occupied himself with transcribing books into his system for the school library and with writing letters to his former pupils. He obtained books or

In 1848, revolutions in France and Europe caught Braille and his friends in their excitement. In Paris, workers and students constructed barricades. With the soldiers of the French national guard, they declared France a republic and toppled King Louis Philippe from the throne he had held for eighteen years.

writing instruments for them at his own expense. He asked students to copy books and, paying them from his own money, then gave the books to others who needed them.

Braille was also generous with his own friends. He kept a small box with his savings in his room. Often a friend or student would come in need of a loan for books for school equipment or tuition for school. Braille seldom denied their request. He would simply note how much they borrowed. When they eventually had the money, Braille knew they would repay him. He even provided scholarships for blind students needing tuition.

Braille's friends tell us of many kind acts performed by this gentle man who never seemed to want to be thanked. He did these things because he felt they were needed and because he wished to do them, not because he wanted people to notice them. He even gave up his job as organist in one of the Paris churches to a colleague who had no job.

Three happy years

Braille survived the bad attack of tuberculosis that year, and the long rest seemed to be helping. By 1847, Allibert thought he could start teaching again, and Dufau allowed him to do so.

A teacher again! And even if he was short of energy and easily exhausted and his chest was delicate, it was still a three-year period of happiness. He conducted his lessons with zest and imagination and continued concentrating his creative energies on the problem of using braille to write music. He also visited his family in Coupvray. As early as 1847, new printing methods adapted to braille were tried out at the school. In all areas of education, braille was beginning to show its suitability and flexibility.

"Despite his blindness, despite continual ill-health, despite the ill-will of others which delayed the recognition of his work, in the face of adversity and of accumulated disappointment he remained kindly, cheerful and faithful to his friends and to his ideal."
Jean Roblin,
Louis Braille

Braille's last years

By 1850, Braille felt that his strength was finally leaving him. He asked to be allowed to retire from teaching. Instead, the director offered to keep him and employ him for a few rare piano lessons.

By December of 1851, Braille knew he was dying. He was not yet forty-three years old. Coltat tells us of severe internal bleeding on the night of December 4. Outside the school, barricades were thrown up on the streets of Paris, and there was fighting on the boulevards. Inside, more internal bleeding confined Braille to his bed for what little was left of his life.

In that same calm, methodical, and thoughtful way he had conducted his whole life, he put his affairs in order. He left his belongings at the institution to Coltat, who distributed them as mementos to his pupils. He arranged that his mother should receive the rest of his property.

Braille died on January 6, 1852, two days after his forty-third birthday. His friends, students, and the many others who had loved him and had felt the benefit of his honest, loving, intelligent nature were going to miss him.

Braille was buried at Coupvray. His body was taken back along the same route that he had traveled thirty-three years earlier when he had made his first journey to the institution where he would achieve his life's work.

"He remembered the little boy who used to guide him, the orderly who nursed him, the night-nurse who sat up with him and even the servant who cleaned his room. On the brink of death, as in his life, he was grateful to those who had helped him."
Jean Roblin,
Louis Braille

"His thirty years of painstaking research had done more for blind people than centuries of alms-giving and charity, and yet Braille died as simply as he had lived, uneulogized and unsung, unknown by his contemporaries."
Jean Roblin,
Louis Braille

But the recognition of Louis Braille's work outside the institution was still to come. Within the next three decades, he would gain fame throughout the world as the greatest champion of blind people. His work allowed millions of blind people to enter a different life because they could read, write, communicate, learn, and create. Because of his efforts, they could take their rightful place in society as cultured and educated human beings.

Braille spreads beyond France

Two years later, in 1854, France formally adopted braille as its official system for blind people. Then the system began to spread outside France. But many people still believed any alphabet for blind people should be based on the alphabet for sighted people. It was hard to convince the teachers of blind people to abandon this belief.

In the 1850s, teachers in French-speaking Switzerland first began to teach braille. In 1860, the Swiss school for blind people at Lausanne printed the first book in braille outside France. German-speaking countries, by contrast, would take forty years before they adopted Braille's dot system.

In England, the process was particularly slow. There were many systems of printing developed for blind people — in the ten years following Braille's basic work on his system, there seems to have been at least twenty methods tried. With few exceptions, they were based on some variation of embossed letters of the ordinary alphabet.

And blind people could work only with the system they had learned. They could not understand material produced in another reading system. Plus, the various other methods were only ways of printing and reading — people could not write with them.

Dr. Thomas Armitage, founder of the British and Foreign Association for Promoting the Education of the Blind, was positive that blind people were the only people qualified to decide upon a single system. He organized a committee of blind people to judge the various methods and select the best. They chose braille. By 1883, most British schools for blind people had adopted it.

International recognition

In 1878, there was a major step forward. An important international congress of European nations — Austria, Hungary, Belgium, Denmark, Britain, France, Germany, Holland, Italy, Sweden, and Switzerland — was held in Paris. It had evaluated the various methods of printing and writing in order to establish a single, unified system worldwide. By a large majority, the congress voted for braille.

But the United States continued to work with a number of systems. These included forms of embossed alphabets, original braille, and at one point, several forms of modified braille. One dot system altered Braille's original idea so that the most frequently used letters had the least number of dots. Another turned Braille's grid of dots on its side so that the grid was longer than it was tall. Such variety in dot systems created confusion. Schoolbooks and other texts had to be printed in three different braille grades. It took almost another forty years before the United States adopted only classic, original braille!

Left: Louis' own watch — the glass can be lifted to feel the hands.

Above: A braille watch, using Louis' six-dot code.

In 1929, eighteen nations adopted an international braille musical notation. This would have delighted Louis Braille, who had spent so many years working to extend his dot notation to music.

In 1932, delegates from nearly a hundred nations accepted a revised form of British braille. Within a short time, it would be possible for almost any English-speaking blind person to write to any other and to read any braille-printed book, newspaper, pamphlet, or magazine.

Now braille has been extended to Indian dialects, Arabic languages, Japanese, Indo-Chinese languages, Chinese, and a number of African dialects.

Modern technology

In 1837, when the institution produced the first book ever printed in braille, the book on the history of France, only one kind of type was made for it. This type contained all six dots. The pupils and tutors chiseled off all of the dots not needed for each of the individual letters. In this way, they made the different types for all the a's, b's, c's, and so on. These were then assembled into words.

The books were large and thick, made up of pages stuck back to back, with the dots protruding outward in the same way that the letters stood out on the pages of embossed Haüy type. It was a long, slow process to put a manuscript into print. But by 1849, there were experiments in printing using stereotyping, which uses whole sheets of metal containing all the embossed symbols for a page.

Today it is possible to use both sides of the paper and both sides of the printing plate through what is called "interpointing." This is a slight shift in the position of the dots on the second side so that they do not coincide with the dots on the first side. This way fingers reading one side of the sheet are not confused.

Another major development was the invention of the braille writer by Frank Hall in the United States. This machine had six keys, one for each dot. You operated this machine by pressing several keys at the same time to make all the dots in any one letter with a single action — a little like striking a chord on a piano. Writing braille by hand, it is difficult to go faster than fifty or sixty letters a minute. But with the braille writer, you can work at twice that speed with little tiredness. Researchers developed typesetting machinery for printing along the same lines and showed models at the Chicago World's Fair in 1893.

Braille in the computer age

In an effort to save space and increase the speed with which braille can be read and written, people have developed a variety of abbreviations and shortened forms of commonly occurring words to supplement the original alphabet. In a contracted version of braille, certain individual letters are given the value of a group of letters. These letters are then used as part of a word or a whole word.

But a sighted person trained in braille was always needed for transcribing books into the dot alphabet. In the late 1950s, researchers in the United States developed braille printing aided by computer.

For the first time, someone who was not skilled in producing braille could produce the type needed. Modern word processors now help the machines. This increases the ease, speed, and accuracy with which manuscripts can be set, altered, and corrected on computers before the metal plates are embossed.

More recently, researchers have developed machines that can electronically read a text printed in ink into a braille production system aided by computers. It can be done four times faster than it can when someone types it at a keyboard — and without any human typing error!

In the future, printers may send material on electronic tape directly to a library or other organization. The library will have an embossing device that will transcribe the electronic tape into braille. Blind readers will then be able to have any braille material they desire.

Personal computers also have opened up enormous possibilities. There are machines and programs that allow a blind person to write, proofread, and correct writing using a braille keyboard and braille display. Blind people can obtain printed copy not just in braille, but also in ordinary ink-print type for sighted people.

An example of the Moon system, developed by Dr. William Moon. Of all the written systems competing with braille in the 1860s, it is the only one that still survives. Because people who lost their sight in their middle or later years are already accustomed to the ordinary alphabet, some people use this method today. They find it easier to use a system like Moon that is based on a modified alphabet rather than to learn a completely new system.

Opposite, above: After the acceptance of braille by an international conference of nations in 1878, several inventors in different countries worked on developing machines for writing braille. Here a blind man is writing with Mauler's braille machine of 1887.

Opposite, below: Students using a braille globe.

Above: A South African man reading a braille version of the Bible.

Right: A blind Nigerian girl is shown a braille tape measure. Braille can be adapted for any language using the Roman alphabet as long as it does not have more than one accent per letter. It can also be adapted for most non-Roman alphabets. At present it has been adapted for more than fifty languages and dialects.

One of France's heroes

A hundred years after Braille's death, the gift of that fifteen-year-old boy who first devised the six-dot system was formally acknowledged as an invention of worldwide significance. In June of 1952, representatives from forty nations came to pay their respects to Louis Braille at his grave in Coupvray. Then they accompanied his body on its last journey to Paris — to the Panthéon to be buried among other great people of France.

One thing is certain. Whether buried in the Panthéon or in his village of Coupvray, Louis Braille's name is unlikely ever to be forgotten.

As long as there are blind people using braille to share in the intellectual heritage of the world and to live as equals alongside sighted people — educated and independent as Louis Braille dreamed they could be — his name will be remembered.

Upper left: A student learning to use braille typewriters at a school for blind people. Some braille typewriters type letters in braille and others type in normal script. Blind people can usually write at a rate of about ten words per minute by hand, but they can double this speed with a mechanical braille writer with six keys.

Lower left: Braille playing cards with the numbers written in the six-dot code.

Questions you may have about blindness

What does it mean to say someone is blind?
There is a legal definition for blindness. It says that people are legally blind if they can see less at twenty feet (6 m) than a person with normal vision can see at two hundred feet (60 m). For example, a blind person can only see the big letter E at the top of the eye chart.

Can people who are legally blind see anything at all?
Most people who are legally blind can see something. Some see light or colors or large or moving objects. Others see things straight in front of them or things to the side of them.

What does it mean to say someone is visually impaired?
People are considered visually impaired if they cannot see and read newspaper type.

How does blindness happen?
Some people are born blind. Others lose their sight gradually later in life or suddenly through disease or accident. The memory of what they could once see helps these people perceive the world around them.

Can blind people hear better than sighted people?
No, a blind person's hearing or other senses are no different than anyone else's. But blind people train themselves to use these senses more because they need them more than a sighted person does. For example, if you close your eyes, you will probably be more aware of what your hearing and your senses of touch and smell can tell you.

Are there other special aids besides books printed in braille for blind or visually impaired people?
Yes. For people who have some vision, there are large-print books in most libraries, hand-held magnifiers, and devices that enlarge the size of a television screen.

People who cannot use their eyes at all for reading have other ways to read. Talking Books are records or tapes that contain a whole book, sped up to go faster than normal speech. Blind people become used to the speed and understand it. Talking computers are also becoming more available and less expensive.

There are braille watches, braille telephones, talking alarm clocks, talking scales, and key rings that beep when you clap your hands. But two of the most useful pieces of equipment for people with visual handicaps are ones sighted people rely on as well, the typewriter and the tape recorder.

What should I do when I meet a blind person?
Introduce yourself just the way you would to anyone else. If you want to shake hands, say something like, "Shall we shake hands?" If the person extends his or her hand first, be sure to take it or explain why you can't. Don't just leave it hanging there. Talk in your normal voice. Most blind people have normal hearing. If the blind person is with someone else, don't ignore him or her and talk only to the companion.

What if I use language involving sight, like "Let's look at both sides of the issue," or "Do you see what I mean?"
Don't worry about it. These phrases have more than one meaning and blind people use them too.

For More Information . . .

Organizations

The organizations listed below have information about Braille, blindness, and people who are visually impaired. Many of them also have state and local branches in addition to the national offices listed here, so check your local phone book. You may be able to call or visit an office in your hometown. When you write or call these organizations, make sure you tell them exactly what you want to know.

American Council of the Blind
1010 Vermont Avenue NW, Suite 1100
Washington, DC 20005

Braille Institute
741 North Vermont Avenue
Los Angeles, CA 90029

National Library Services for the
  Blind and Physically Handicapped
Library of Congress
1291 Taylor Street NW
Washington, DC 20542

Canadian Council of the Blind
220 Dundas Street, Suite 510
London, Ontario N6A 1H3

Canadian National Institute for the Blind
1931 Bayview Avenue
Toronto, Ontario M4G 4C8

Association for the Education and Rehabilitation
  of the Blind and Visually Impaired
206 N. Washington Street, Suite 320
Alexandria, VA 22314

Places to Visit

Listed below are some places you can visit with exhibits and information on Braille and on people who are blind or visually impaired. You can also write to these places if you want more information.

American Foundation for the Blind
15 West 16th Street
New York, NY 10011

American Printing House for the Blind
P.O. Box 6085
1839 Frankfort Avenue
Louisville, KY 40206

Columbia Lighthouse for the Blind
1421 P Street NW
Washington, DC 20005

National Federation of the Blind
1800 Johnson Street
Baltimore, MD 21230

Books

These books will help you learn more about Braille and his system and about people who are blind or visually impaired. Check your local library or bookstore to see if they have them or if someone there will order them for you.

Child of the Silent Night: The Story of Laura Bridgeman. Hunter (Houghton Mifflin)
Connie's New Eyes. Wolf (Lippincott Junior)
Feeling Free. Sullivan (Addison-Wesley)
If You Could See What I Hear. Sullivan and Gill (New American Library)

Louis Braille. Keeler (Franklin Watts)
The Miracle Worker. Gibson (Bantam)
My Mother Is Blind. Reuter (Childrens Press)
The New Boy Is Blind. Thomas (Messner)
Seeing in Special Ways — Children Living with Blindness. Bergman
    (Gareth Stevens)
The Seeing Summer. Eyerly (Archway)
Seeing Through the Dark: Blind and Sighted, A Vision Shared. Weiss
    (Harcourt Brace Jovanovich)
Shelley's Day: The Day of a Legally Blind Child. Hall (Andrew Mountain)
Through Grandpa's Eyes. MacLachlan (Harper Junior)
To Catch an Angel: Adventures in a World I Cannot See. Russell (Vanguard)
What If You Couldn't . . . ? A Book About Special Needs. Kamien (Scribner's)

Glossary

Abdicate
To resign as ruler.

Antibiotic
A chemical substance, such as penicillin, that can kill the microorganisms that cause disease or prevent them from growing.

Asylum
A place where people, especially disabled people, can lead protected or safe lives.

Awl
A pointed tool used for making holes in wood or leather.

Barricade
A barrier in the street, often built with carts, furniture, paving stones, and anything else nearby. The Parisians were inclined to "go to the barricades" whenever they were unhappy with political events.

Bavaria
A region in the southeastern part of West Germany.

Billet
To lodge soldiers in private houses rather than to have them camp outside.

Bushel
A unit of volume or capacity used to measure liquids and solids. One bushel equals about nine U.S. gallons (35 L).

Cavalrymen
Soldiers who are trained to fight on horseback.

Chamber of Deputies
A branch of the French government in the nineteenth century.

Chateau
A French country house or castle.

Congress

As used in this book, a meeting of experts and other people interested in a particular topic, for example, blindness.

Czar

The emperor of Russia.

Dominoes

A game played with rectangular blocks marked with dots. Played on flat surfaces like tabletops or floors, dominoes was a popular game in Braille's childhood.

Dormitory

A room where several people sleep. The term can also refer to a building that houses people who are working in institutions such as schools.

Germ

A microorganism, especially one that can cause disease.

Grammar

The system of rules that organize the way that people write or speak a language. A grammar book contains these rules.

Hospital of Quinze-Vingts

A hospital for poor blind people originally built in Paris during the mid-thirteenth century. The hospital is still operating today and specializes in eye diseases.

Interpointing

The system of setting braille print so that the dots on one side of the page do not interfere with the dots on the other side.

Microorganism

A living thing made of a single cell and too small to be seen with the naked eye. Bacteria, yeasts, and viruses are examples of microorganisms.

Napoleon Bonaparte

A French leader born in Corsica in 1769. He became the leader of France in 1799 after overthrowing the government. He was a brilliant general, and his armies conquered most of Europe between 1800 and 1813. The British and the Prussians defeated Napoleon at the Battle of Waterloo in 1815. He was sent into exile on the island of St. Helena in the southern Atlantic and died there in 1821.

Pantheon

A building that serves as a memorial or tomb for a country's famous dead people. The Panthéon in Paris was originally named the Church of Saint Genevieve and was designed in 1764.

Penicillin

An antibiotic made from a fungus. It is used to treat a wide variety of infections.

Prussia

A kingdom in present-day northeast Germany and Poland. It became the central country in the German Confederation. In 1871, the king of Prussia became the emperor, or *Kaiser*, of Germany.

Raphigraphy
Braille's name for his method of writing that allowed blind people to write to sighted people. In 1841, François-Pierre Foucault invented a machine for typing raphigraphy.

Saddler
A skilled worker who makes all kinds of equipment, especially saddles, for horses.

Scholarship
Money provided for a student who shows an outstanding ability to learn. Today, some universities also provide scholarships to people with great athletic abilities in specific sports, such as football and basketball.

Sonography
The night writing developed by Captain Charles Barbier for military use. It inspired Braille to develop his own dot alphabet.

Stylus
A sharp, pointed tool for writing, marking, or engraving. Braille used a stylus to prick his dots into paper.

Tuberculosis
A disease that mainly attacks the lungs and is caused by germs. People can catch tuberculosis by drinking milk from infected cows or by breathing in the germs from other people. In damp conditions, these germs can live for weeks in dust and dirt, but sunlight kills them.

Versailles
The name of both a city and the ornate palace located there. The palace has numerous rooms filled with mirrors, paintings, art objects, huge chandeliers, and lavish furniture. Its gardens are famous for their size, design, sculptures, and fountains. Located near Paris, the Versailles palace is now a national museum.

Chronology

1771   **September** — Valentin Haüy sees some people at a fair making fun of blind people. He is appalled and resolves to help blind people.

1784   The Royal Institution for Blind Children, founded by Haüy, opens in Paris.

1786   At Versailles, a group of blind children from the institution gives a demonstration of reading by touch. Louis XVI gives the school some money and his support.

1789   The French Revolution begins. Haüy is dismissed as principal of the school.

1800   On Napoleon's orders, the blind children are put into an asylum for people with other disabilities.

1806   Haüy flees from the turmoil in France with Remy Fournier, one of his students. They go to Prussia and start a school.

1807   As Napoleon's armies advance, Haüy and Fournier escape to Russia and set up another school for blind children.

1809	**January 4** — Louis Braille is born in Coupvray, France.
1812	Louis, age three, blinds one eye in an accident. He gradually loses sight in his other eye as well.
1814	Russian troops occupy Coupvray as Napoleon's empire falls. Captain Barbier starts work on his night-writing system.
1815	Jacques Palluy becomes the parish priest of Coupvray and starts teaching Louis. The Royal Institution for Blind Children reopens in Paris.
1816	Antoine Bécheret offers Louis a place as a student in the Coupvray school.
1819	Louis, age ten, leaves for Paris to attend the school founded by Haüy. Louis learns to play the piano and shows great musical talent.
1821	Barbier demonstrates his night writing to the institution. The students are delighted. Dr. André Pignier becomes the new director.
1824	After about three years of work, Louis completes his first dot alphabet based on Barbier's invention of sonography. He is only fifteen.
1827	A French grammar book is transcribed into Louis' six-dot system.
1828	Braille becomes an assistant teacher at the institution and adapts his system to write music. A panel of doctors condemns the institution building as harmful to the children's health.
1829	Braille publishes a booklet explaining his six-dot system.
1833	Braille gains a position as an organist at a nearby church. He continues working as an organist for the rest of his life.
1834	The governors of the institution refuse to allow the students to use Braille's alphabet. Braille demonstrates his six-dot system at the Exhibition of Industry in Paris.
1835	Braille shows the first symptoms of tuberculosis.
1837	Blind teachers and students at the institution produce the first book in the braille system.
1838	**May 14** — At the French National Assembly, Alphonse Marie Louis de Lamartine condemns the conditions at the institution. The Assembly votes to spend 1.6 million francs for a new building.
1839	Braille starts work with sighted assistants on machines that will print his dot system.
1840	P. Armand Dufau and the school directors force Dr. Pignier to retire. Dufau takes over, destroys all previous books for the blind students, and brings in new systems using embossed letters for reading. Joseph Gaudet becomes his deputy director.
1841	François-Pierre Foucault invents his machine for typing raphigraphy.

1843   Braille's health fails and he goes to Coupvray for six months to recover. **November** — The new school for blind children is finished and the move is completed.

1844   **February 22** — The new school is officially opened. The students give a totally convincing display of the advantages of braille.

1847   Foucault, along with Louis Braille, finishes developing a braille typewriter.

1850   Braille's tuberculosis gets worse and he can give only a few music lessons.

1851   Braille is so ill that he enters the institution's hospital.

1852   **January 6** — Louis Braille dies at age forty-three and is buried in Coupvray.

1854   France adopts braille as its official system for blind people.

1878   An international congress decides braille is the best system for blind people and agrees to promote braille around the world.

1917   The United States accepts braille for general use.

1929   Thirteen nations agree with a conference of five other nations to adopt international braille notation for music.

1949   India asks UNESCO — the United Nations Educational, Scientific, and Cultural Organization — to regulate braille for use in all languages. Over one hundred languages and hundreds of dialects can now be written in braille.

1952   Braille's body is moved from Coupvray and reburied in the Panthéon in Paris — the place of highest honor for any French citizen.

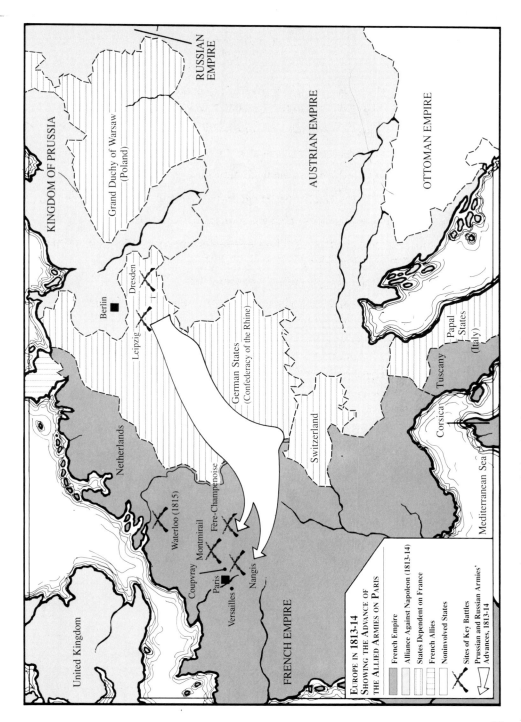

RUSSIAN EMPIRE

KINGDOM OF PRUSSIA

Grand Duchy of Warsaw (Poland)

AUSTRIAN EMPIRE

OTTOMAN EMPIRE

Berlin

Dresden

Leipzig

German States (Confederacy of the Rhine)

Switzerland

Papal States (Italy)

Tuscany

Corsica

Mediterranean Sea

Netherlands

Waterloo (1815)

Montmirail

Fère-Champenoise

Coupvray

Paris

Versailles

Nangis

United Kingdom

FRENCH EMPIRE

EUROPE IN 1813-14
SHOWING THE ADVANCE OF
THE ALLIED ARMIES ON PARIS

French Empire

Alliance Against Napoleon (1813-14)

States Dependent on France

French Allies

Noninvolved States

Sites of Key Battles

Prussian and Russian Armies'
Advances, 1813-14

Index